Finding Your Way

A journal of guided prompts to tap into your inner guidance

Sarah Stecbler

INCLUDED IN THIS GUIDED JOURNAL

Guided prompts and seed sentences guide you through an immersive experience of connecting to the deeper wisdom within you that's often covered up by overwhelm, & day-to-day chaos. Through this process you'll gain clarity, eliminate decision fatigue, and bring yourself back to your highest potential.

This process repeats 4x allowing you to come back to these prompts every quarter or throughout various seasons of your life. Each time you'll notice new insights, reflect on your growth, and improve your outlook and mindset further.

Additional lined pages at the back allow you to dive deeper into prompts that trigger a higher level of insight and awareness.

ADDITIONAL PLANNERS YOU MIGHT ENJOY:

The **Mindful Productivity Planner** is an undated monthly & weekly planner designed to track your habits, create monthly bucket lists, and reflect on each month with guided prompts.

The **Daily Productivity & Brain Dump Book** includes daily structured brain dump pages to declutter your mind and help you prioritize target tasks for the day. The daily productivity page helps you create focus, manage your time & build daily momentum.

Listen to the **Mindful Productivity Podcast** for Free on iTunes, Spotify, and anywhere podcasts are found

Find more resources by visiting MindfulProductivityBlog.com

COPYRIGHT & DISCLAIMER

© 2019 by Sarah Steckler | SARAH OSE COMPANY, LLC

ALL RIGHTS RESERVED. No part of this publication may be reproduced, distributed, or transmitted in any form or by any means, including photocopying, recording, or other electronic or mechanical methods, without the prior written permission of the publisher, except in the case of brief quotations embodied in critical reviews and certain other noncommercial uses permitted by copyright law.

DISCLAIMER OF LIABILITY. The information provided in this book is for general purposes only and should not replace medical, inancial, or professional advice. The author and publisher are not responsible or liable for any outcomes caused by actions taken from this publication. Readers accept full responsibility for any of the actions they take from suggestions within this planner.

CREATIVE CREDIT. Planner content written, created, and designed by Sarah Steckler. Cover fonts & elements by Creativeqube Design used with licensed permission. Interior Title Font by Nicky Laatz used with licensed permission.

Hello!

You're about to dive into an abundance of self-discovery and realizations that may both inspire you and possibly challenge you. In many ways, you are about to take a journey that will lead you to a new way of seeing the world around you. Be patient with your findings and trust in the process.

Through your own words, you'll discover what it truly means to be who you are and the great, endless abundance of gifts, inner guidance, and ability you have before you. Opening yourself up to that kind of trust in yourself is the biggest gift you could receive - and it's a kind of love that radiates endlessly when you step into it with commitment and determination.

So how does this process work? Inside this journal, you'll find a series of prompts divided into four sections. The series of prompts repeat 4x, meaning you'll have four opportunities to repeat the process. These are for you to go through every quarter or season of your life that feels applicable. You'll find that your answers will change and shift over time and by the end of it all, you'll have a little book full of wisdom you can come back to and reference.

Most of these seed sentences are designed to trigger a "rapid-fire" response from you. Go with your gut and write down the first thing that comes into your mind. There is no "best" or "right" answer for these. If you need more space to explore a prompt, head to the back of this journal where you'll find additional lined pages.

Give yourself a couple hours the first go-around. Cozy up with a warm beverage, sink into your favorite chair and indulge in these moments of being fully present with yourself. There are amazing discoveries to be had!

It all started when I knew I couldn't listen anymore. To the endless "*shoulds*" from others and myself. To the nonstop pressure to do one thing over another.

I kept feeling it, deep in my gut, throughout my heart, pounding through my chest, that underneath it all, I truly KNEW what I wanted, needed, and believed in, I just needed to find a way to give it a voice.

Years ago during a performance review someone wrote, "*if she could find her voice, she could truly lead.*"

I never looked back after I read that. It resonated so deeply that from that day forward my ultimate mission was to find my voice.

And I want the same for you.

Because the thing is, when you find your voice, you come to know yourself in a way that brings power to your decisions, ease to your choices, consistency to your habits, confidence to your mind, and love to your very being.

Voice isn't merely about how loud you shout, it's how quietly you can whisper and still be heard. It's about an awareness so deep, that you don't feel the need to waver when it comes to your self-care and doing what feels aligned, raw, and true to your core.

You owe it to yourself and the world around you to breathe your force with each breath.

And over the course of however you decide to make your way through these prompts. You'll do just that.

Sarah Stecbler

These prompts will serve as your guide of discovery, allowing you to open up new realms of possibility, dive deeply into self-awareness, and uncover moments of bliss and inner guidance that you've always had within you.

Bite them off with enough time to chew or slowly savor. There is no rush. There is no finish line in terms of going through these. You may find they are best used at the start of the day or most savored in the evening with tea. Work them into your routine as you feel called to. You may also wish to bring them on a trip, devour them in a matter of hours, or share them with friends at a get-together.

This is the ritual I have created that has allowed me to step fully into trusting in my own decisions, the process of how I think and observe, and what ultimately makes me feel aligned with a choice.

You will notice that your answers to them may change depending on many variables, allow yourself to waver, swing, and flow through them with these variations. All of your answers will hold truth, lessons, and meaning.

Some tips to ease your mind:

- Allow yourself to respond with your intuition or gut feeling. Worry less about writing the "best" answer and instead focus on what comes up for you. Sometimes simple responses yield powerful realizations.
- Start from where you are. The present moment is the only moment you can be in. Revel in it. *(If you need additional support here, listen to Episode 1 of the Mindful Productivity Podcast).*

Additional ways to use these prompts and reflect on your responses:

- Choose a time to go through these each year and look back on your answers
- Choose a section or theme that calls to you
- Fill them out randomly or in the systematic way as I've provided
- Add the prompts to a jar and pull one daily
- Bring them along on a trip or retreat and share them with friends
- Discuss, share, or marvel in how your answers appear and change over time
- You may find at times that some prompts require more journaling to deeply expand on your thoughts. I encourage you to do whatever feels best for your self-discovery here.

Affirmation of self trust

I _____, choose to honor and respect my mind, growth, and mental well-being.

I give myself permission to start from where I am without judgement, resentment, or hurried intention.

I welcome the slow growth, the possibility of rapid awareness, and know that I have always have a choice to move at a pace that best serves me.

I welcome the challenge and possible struggle that comes with diving deeper into uncovering who I am at this time in my life and trust in my higher self to guide me as needed.

I understand that simply reading this guide will not change my way of thinking but that devoting time to myself and these prompts will help direct me into trusting my own inner voice.

Ninety percent of the world's woes comes from people not knowing themselves, their abilities, their frailties, and even their real virtues. Most of us go almost all the way through life as complete strangers to ourselves.
-Sidney J. Harris

From Where I begin

I am starting this journal on _____

I am currently _____ years old but I feel more like _____
and I think it's because _____
_____
_____

One thing I know for sure is that I am _____
and it allows me to _____

My hope is to discover _____

The biggest struggle for me right now is _____
and it often causes _____

The 3 things I am most happy about at this time:
1)_____
2)_____
3)_____

3 Things I know now that I didn't know a year ago:
1)_____
2)_____
3)_____

I know that if I choose to let go of _____
I will give myself freedom in the form of _____

Reflection

Last year around this time I was struggling with _____ and now I'm confident in _____

6 months ago I used to _____, now I
_____

I don't give myself enough credit for how often I
_____

I now realize that my relationship with _____ is/was causing _____

I found that many of my thoughts were focused on _____ _____and I'd like to shift them toward
_____

I know I have experienced growth because _____
_____
and it shows in how I _____

I find myself _____ much less and
_____much more.

If I had to choose a word or a theme for the past year, it would be _____ because _____
_____

Take Pause

Now that you've taken some time to reflect on your growth and awareness, take a deep breath and let it all marinate for a moment. You may want to put down this workbook and go for a walk or set a timer for 5 minutes to meditate or have a glass of water. Once you feel collected, use the space below to narrow your focus.

I have realized that I want to feel more _____ in my life because _____

Now more than ever, it is important that I focus on _____

I had no idea just how much _____ was affecting my daily life.

Circle the areas of your life below that feel good. Highlight the ones that you want to fuel, nourish, and grow.

Self-Love   Family   Friends   Boundaries   Support

Home   Health   Movement   Sleep   Self-Care   Relaxation

Trust   Work   Creativity   Spirituality   Organization

Nourishment   Environment   Emotional   Fun   Nature

Find Your Focus

As you continue through this guide you have several choices. To journey through it without barriers or to answer the remaining prompts with a specific lens in line with your goals and focus areas. There is no wrong or right way to continue. The beauty is that you can use this guide over and over again in a variety of ways. If you're craving more structure, the next few pages are for you.

Use the space below to write down the words you have highlighted on the previous page.

Find Your Focus Continued

This next step will help you get clear on which areas of your life you feel most energetically drawn to, in other words, the areas that you're feeling in your gut need your attention now more than ever. This part can be a bit tricky but I'm going to ask you to narrow down your choices to only two areas.

Area 1

What is lacking? What do you ultimately want? What changes if that happens for you?

_____
_____
_____
_____
_____
_____
_____
_____

Area 2

What is lacking? What do you ultimately want? What changes if that happens for you?

_____
_____
_____
_____
_____
_____
_____
_____

Harnessing Your Power

Congratulations, you're about to choose a focus! There may still be some resistance for you here and that's normal. Focusing in now will not limit you, it will help you gain a deep understanding and clarity on each area and section of your life in great detail. This gives you the power to eliminate confusion, self-doubt, and all of those nasty "what ifs" that can keep us up late at night. Once you have become clear on one at a time you can come back through this process once more. Go head, announce it, already!

I am choosing to focus on _____ and I know it's time because _____

I feel _____ and that's okay.

One thing I know for sure is that committing to this area of my life will allow me to finally _____ and _____

I am looking forward to this area allowing me to _____ and step into

_____

I am afraid that diving deeper into this area of my life might mean _____ but I trust that _____

_____

Use this space to let go of any additional thoughts, worries, or concerns you need to release at this moment. This allows you to rid yourself of mental clutter and better focus on what you truly need. Do not worry about trying to solve them, simply write them down.

_____
_____
_____
_____
_____
_____
_____
_____
_____
_____
_____
_____
_____
_____
_____
_____
_____
_____
_____
_____
_____
_____
_____
_____
_____
_____
_____
_____
_____
_____

Beginnings

The hardest part about starting is _____
but it's easier when I _____

I am confident that if I _____
that I will be successful in _____

Right now it is important that I _____
so I can focus on
_____

I am looking for _____
and I can find it by _____

I feel overwhelmed by the idea of _____
but I give myself permission to _____

In starting from where I am without judgment, I will be able
to _____

The biggest lie I keep telling myself is _____
and I've proven it's not true by _____

When I get overwhelmed I tend to _____
and I can take care of myself and this feeling by _____
_____

Belief consists in accepting the affirmations of the soul; unbelief, in denying them.
-Ralph Waldo Emerson

Preparation

It's important that I feel _____
in order to feel confident getting started.

In the past, it has been helpful to _____
before jumping into a new goal.

The biggest reason I want to _____
is to allow myself to _____

I feel less stressed when I _____
which allows me to _____

One way I could start tracking my to-do list is to _____
and then reward myself by _____

Everything I want to work on would feel a lot less overwhelming
if I made time to _____

I can create structure toward my desires by _____
and I will make this a priority by _____

A few things that I need help and direction on are _____
_____
and I can get help and find resource for this by _____
_____

When I've lost my way or when I am confused about a path to take, I remember that most answers I need I already possess deep inside. I am naturally creative, resourceful and whole. If I consult my invisible compass, I'll know what to do.
— Steve Goodier

Intuition

I know something is off when I feel _____
_____in my body.

There have been times my gut feeling has tried to tell me
_____ and I ignored it which led to
_____

The last time I trusted in my gut feeling, I _____
and it showed me _____

I often seek external validation in the form of _____
and it has made me feel _____

I also find that seeking external validation can cause me to
_____ and prevent me from
_____

There are times when I have to trust in myself over the
opinions or words of others, I can best do this by _____
_____

I don't need facts or hard logic to know when I _____
because _____

Trusting in myself means allowing myself to _____
even in the face of _____

Decision

When I feel overwhelmed by choice, it usually stems from a fear of _____

The biggest decision I ever made was _____
_____ and it helped me discover _____
_____

Choices feel difficult when I'm not paying attention to
_____
and I can change this by _____

I can trust myself more to make decisions that serve me by
_____

When in doubt, the best things that help me weigh my options are _____

Taking time to let go of others' expectations helps me make decisions rooted in _____
instead of _____

When I feel indecisive, it's important that I take time to
_____ and give myself enough time to
_____

Trust

It is important that I take time to _____
in a new relationship before I _____

I trust in my ability to _____
for myself because I know _____

If I spoke the words I speak to myself to others, I would feel
_____ about how they were
being treated.

When I feel I need advice and no one is around, I know I can
take time to _____
and it will give me the answers that I need.

In order for me to feel comfortable being my true self in front of
others, I need to know _____
and I will know this by _____

I know that I cannot trust someone when _____
and I often have to remind myself of this by _____
_____

For me, trust means _____
and it's important that I keep this standard to myself because
_____

Connection

I find that I _____ need to be around people for _____ amount of time in order to feel like my best self.

When I think of community, I think of _____

I thrive when I am _____ people for an extended period of time.

Alone time makes me feel _____ and time with others makes me feel _____

Feeling connected means that I feel _____ and this usually happens when _____

I feel most connected to myself when I am _____ and the last time I made time for this was _____

As I look ahead, it's important that I find connection for myself by _____ and reflecting on _____

I feel most alone when _____ and most connected when _____

When I think about the connections I currently have in life, in awareness, in creativity, and so forth, I want to make more time for _____

Acceptance

I am working on accepting that I _____
and it is helping me to see that _____

Acceptance means that I allow myself to _____
even in the face of _____

I am learning to _____ the things I
cannot change and _____
with the aspects of life that I can shift.

When things don't go my way I want to _____
_____
instead of _____

I will be able to make this a reality by regularly _____
_____

When I encounter things I cannot accept, I will assert my
boundaries by _____
and by honoring _____

To me, there is a big difference between acceptance and
_____. This distinction helps me see
_____

Creativity

Happiness researchers have discovered that we enter happy zones when we are focused and in the moment on a specific task. It's why knitting, drawing, coloring, crafting, or even playing strategic video games can make us feel at ease and enthralled in the process. Creating is important but the process of creating and being present can be even more so. Whatever you create, no matter how tactile, abstract, or imaginary, creates purpose in the process, and a deeply rooted sense of self-worth and self-efficacy is hidden in there as well. I encourage you to take time to create, not for the finished product alone, but also for the enjoyment of creating.

Creating for me means _____
and feeling _____
in the process.

I have always enjoyed the process of _____
and looking back I think it's because it truly allowed me to be able to _____
_____

Top projects I've LOVED the process of:
_____
_____
_____
_____

Mindset

I tend to assume that I cannot _____
and it has limited me when _____
_____

I regularly tell myself _____
when starting a new challenge.

If I truly believed that I could _____
big things would change in how I _____
_____

My ability to _____
shows up in how I _____

When I doubt myself or my abilities, it's helpful to take time
to reflect on _____
and then take action by _____

I find a lot of comfort in _____
which can often hinder my ability to _____

I now choose to believe that I _____
and this will help me in _____
_____

Huddle

Holy moly, that was a lot of introspective work. I don't know about you but the first few times I went through these, I needed to give my mind some time to exhale and take five. For that reason, this next section is geared to help you reset your brain -- kind of like smelling coffee beans after you smell too much perfume at Macy's.

I also love making lists like this to come back to years later. So if you use this on a yearly or regular basis, you'll have a ton of fun seeing how your answers change over time.

Currently, I'm...

Reading _____
Watching _____
Celebrating _____
Obsessed with _____
Wanting _____
Thinking about _____
Deciding _____
Feeling nostalgic _____
Wondering if _____
Debating _____
Craving _____
Creating _____
Dreaming _____
Brainstorming _____

Big Takeaways

Time to get real with yourself. What just happened back there? What's new? What has changed for you? What are you aware of now that you weren't before? Gush out all of the details here and make sure you get those juicy highlights down..........dang!

Looking Back

How did your area of focus effect your answers to the prompts?

_____
_____
_____
_____
_____

List out additional themes, words, or ideas that came to you during this process.

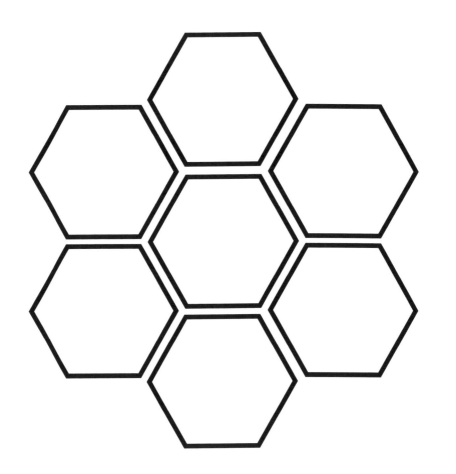

Looking Ahead

Real talk. This journal could have been hundreds of pages if I had let it. The truth is that you've just discovered 99% of what you need to know about yourself to keep the momentum going. And if I tried to get you through another 900 whatever pages of prompts, you'd probably give up, think I was crazy, or burn this book.

So let's bring it in real close for a moment to get clear on one thing.

YOU HAVE ALL THE ANSWERS INSIDE OF YOU

No one else on this planet can tell you what YOU need for YOU, except you. I'm not saying you shouldn't consult medical professionals, mental health specialists, financial advisors, or whoever is the expert in the advice you may be seeking. But what I am saying is that when it comes down to making a CHOICE about which direction to go with the information at your fingertips, the best person to turn to is yourself.

And the best way to build that trust and self-assurance in yourself and your own inner guidance is to touch base from time to time. Take yourself out on some sweet solo dates, bask in your awareness, and venture deep into journaling and self-discovery.

Momentum

What felt good during this process?

_____
_____
_____
_____

What needs more attention?

_____
_____
_____
_____

What are you ultimately seeking now?

_____
_____

What 3 daily steps/habits/practices can you start to make that happen?

_____
_____

How often do you want to come back to your reflections here? How will you remind yourself?

_____
_____

Take 2
_____

We have more possibilities available in each moment than we realize.
-Thich Nhat Hanh

From Where I begin

I am starting this journal on _____

I am currently _____ years old but I feel more like _____
and I think it's because _____
_____
_____

One thing I know for sure is that I am _____
and it allows me to _____

My hope is to discover _____

The biggest struggle for me right now is _____
and it often causes _____

The 3 things I am most happy about at this time:
1)_____
2)_____
3)_____

3 Things I know now that I didn't know a year ago:
1)_____
2)_____
3)_____

I know that if I choose to let go of _____
I will give myself freedom in the form of _____

Reflection

Last year around this time I was struggling with _____ and now I'm confident in _____

6 months ago I used to _____, now I _____ _____

I don't give myself enough credit for how often I _____

I now realize that my relationship with _____ is/was causing _____

I found that many of my thoughts were focused on _____ _____and I'd like to shift them toward _____

I know I have experienced growth because _____ _____ and it shows in how I _____

I find myself _____ much less and _____much more.

If I had to choose a word or a theme for the past year, it would be _____ because _____ _____

Take Pause

Now that you've taken some time to reflect on your growth and awareness, take a deep breath and let it all marinate for a moment. You may want to put down this workbook and go for a walk or set a timer for 5 minutes to meditate or have a glass of water. Once you feel collected, use the space below to narrow your focus.

I have realized that I want to feel more _____ in my life because _____

Now more than ever, it is important that I focus on
_____
_____

I had no idea just how much _____ was affecting my daily life.

Circle the areas of your life below that feel good. Highlight the ones that you want to fuel, nourish, and grow.

Self-Love   Family   Friends   Boundaries   Support

Home   Health   Movement   Sleep   Self-Care   Relaxation

Trust   Work   Creativity   Spirituality   Organization

Nourishment   Environment   Emotional   Fun   Nature

Find Your Focus

As you continue through this guide you have several choices. To journey through it without barriers or to answer the remaining prompts with a specific lens in line with your goals and focus areas. There is no wrong or right way to continue. The beauty is that you can use this guide over and over again in a variety of ways. If you're craving more structure, the next few pages are for you.

Use the space below to write down the words you have highlighted on the previous page.

Find Your Focus Continued

This next step will help you get clear on which areas of your life you feel most energetically drawn to, in other words, the areas that you're feeling in your gut need your attention now more than ever. This part can be a bit tricky but I'm going to ask you to narrow down your choices to only two areas.

Area 1

What is lacking? What do you ultimately want? What changes if that happens for you?

_____
_____
_____
_____
_____
_____
_____
_____

Area 2

What is lacking? What do you ultimately want? What changes if that happens for you?

_____
_____
_____
_____
_____
_____
_____
_____

Harnessing Your Power

Congratulations, you're about to choose a focus! There may still be some resistance for you here and that's normal. Focusing in now will not limit you, it will help you gain a deep understanding and clarity on each area and section of your life in great detail. This gives you the power to eliminate confusion, self-doubt, and all of those nasty "what ifs" that can keep us up late at night. Once you have become clear on one at a time you can come back through this process once more. Go head, announce it, already!

I am choosing to focus on _____
and I know it's time because _____

I feel _____ and that's okay.

One thing I know for sure is that committing to this area of my life will allow me to finally _____
and _____

I am looking forward to this area allowing me to _____
and step into _____

I am afraid that diving deeper into this area of my life might mean _____
but I trust that _____
_____

Use this space to let go of any additional thoughts, worries, or concerns you need to release at this moment. This allows you to rid yourself of mental clutter and better focus on what you truly need. Do not worry about trying to solve them, simply write them down.

Beginnings

The hardest part about starting is _____
but it's easier when I _____

I am confident that if I _____
that I will be successful in _____

Right now it is important that I _____
so I can focus on _____

I am looking for _____
and I can find it by _____

I feel overwhelmed by the idea of _____
but I give myself permission to _____

In starting from where I am without judgment, I will be able
to _____

The biggest lie I keep telling myself is _____
and I've proven it's not true by _____

When I get overwhelmed I tend to _____
and I can take care of myself and this feeling by _____
_____

Let go of who you think you're supposed to be; embrace who you are.

-Brene Brown

Preparation

It's important that I feel _____
in order to feel confident getting started.

In the past, it has been helpful to _____
before jumping into a new goal.

The biggest reason I want to _____
is to allow myself to_____

I feel less stressed when I _____
which allows me to _____

One way I could start tracking my to-do list is to _____
and then reward myself by _____

Everything I want to work on would feel a lot less overwhelming
if I made time to _____

I can create structure toward my desires by _____
and I will make this a priority by _____

A few things that I need help and direction on are _____
_____
and I can get help and find resource for this by _____
_____

When I've lost my way or when I am confused about a path to take, I remember that most answers I need I already possess deep inside. I am naturally creative, resourceful and whole. If I consult my invisible compass, I'll know what to do.
— Steve Goodier

Intuition

I know something is off when I feel _____
_____ in my body.

There have been times my gut feeling has tried to tell me
_____ and I ignored it which led to
_____

The last time I trusted in my gut feeling, I _____
and it showed me _____

I often seek external validation in the form of _____
and it has made me feel _____

I also find that seeking external validation can cause me to
_____ and prevent me from
_____

There are times when I have to trust in myself over the
opinions or words of others, I can best do this by _____
_____

I don't need facts or hard logic to know when I _____
because _____

Trusting in myself means allowing myself to _____
even in the face of _____

Decision

When I feel overwhelmed by choice, it usually stems from a fear of _____

The biggest decision I ever made was _____ _____ and it helped me discover _____ _____

Choices feel difficult when I'm not paying attention to _____
and I can change this by _____

I can trust myself more to make decisions that serve me by _____

When in doubt, the best things that help me weigh my options are _____

Taking time to let go of others' expectations helps me make decisions rooted in _____
instead of _____

When I feel indecisive, it's important that I take time to _____ and give myself enough time to _____

Trust

It is important that I take time to _____
in a new relationship before I _____

I trust in my ability to _____
for myself because I know _____

If I spoke the words I speak to myself to others, I would feel
_____ about how they were
being treated.

When I feel I need advice and no one is around, I know I can
take time to _____
and it will give me the answers that I need.

In order for me to feel comfortable being my true self in front of
others, I need to know
_____
and I will know this by _____

I know that I cannot trust someone when _____
and I often have to remind myself of this by _____
_____

For me, trust means _____
and it's important that I keep this standard to myself because
_____

Connection

I find that I _____ need to be around people for _____ amount of time in order to feel like my best self.

When I think of community, I think of _____

I thrive when I am _____ people for an extended period of time.

Alone time makes me feel _____ and time with others makes me feel _____

Feeling connected means that I feel _____ and this usually happens when _____

I feel most connected to myself when I am _____ and the last time I made time for this was _____
_____

As I look ahead, it's important that I find connection for myself by _____
and reflecting on _____

I feel most alone when _____
and most connected when _____

When I think about the connections I currently have in life, in awareness, in creativity, and so forth, I want to make more time for _____

Acceptance

I am working on accepting that I _____
and it is helping me to see that _____

Acceptance means that I allow myself to _____
even in the face of _____

I am learning to _____ the things I
cannot change and _____
with the aspects of life that I can shift.

When things don't go my way I want to _____
_____
instead of _____

I will be able to make this a reality by regularly _____
_____

When I encounter things I cannot accept, I will assert my
boundaries by _____
and by honoring _____

To me, there is a big difference between acceptance and
_____. This distinction helps me see
_____

Creativity

Happiness researchers have discovered that we enter happy zones when we are focused and in the moment on a specific task. It's why knitting, drawing, coloring, crafting, or even playing strategic video games can make us feel at ease and enthralled in the process. Creating is important but the process of creating and being present can be even more so. Whatever you create, no matter how tactile, abstract, or imaginary, creates purpose in the process, and a deeply rooted sense of self-worth and self-efficacy is hidden in there as well. I encourage you to take time to create, not for the finished product alone, but also for the enjoyment of creating.

Creating for me means _____
and feeling _____
in the process.

I have always enjoyed the process of _____
and looking back I think it's because it truly allowed me to be able to _____
_____

Top projects I've LOVED the process of

_____
_____
_____
_____

Mindset

I tend to assume that I cannot _____
and it has limited me when _____
_____

I regularly tell myself _____
when starting a new challenge.

If I truly believed that I could _____
big things would change in how I _____
_____

My ability to _____
shows up in how I _____

When I doubt myself or my abilities, it's helpful to take time
to reflect on _____
and then take action by _____

I find a lot of comfort in _____
which can often hinder my ability to _____

I now choose to believe that I _____
and this will help me in _____
_____

Huddle

Holy moly, that was a lot of introspective work. I don't know about you but the first few times I went through these, I needed to give my mind some time to exhale and take five. For that reason, this next section is geared to help you reset your brain -- kind of like smelling coffee beans after you smell too much perfume at Macy's.

I also love making lists like this to come back to years later. So if you use this on a yearly or regular basis, you'll have a ton of fun seeing how your answers change over time.

Currently, I'm...

Reading _____
Watching _____
Celebrating _____
Obsessed with _____
Wanting _____
Thinking about _____
Deciding _____
Feeling nostalgic _____
Wondering if _____
Debating _____
Craving _____
Creating _____
Dreaming _____
Brainstorming _____

Big Takeaways

Time to get real with yourself. What just happened back there? What's new? What has changed for you? What are you aware of now that you weren't before? Gush out all of the details here and make sure you get those juicy highlights down..........dang!

Looking Back

How did your area of focus effect your answers to the prompts?

_____
_____
_____
_____
_____

List out additional themes, words, or ideas that came to you during this process.

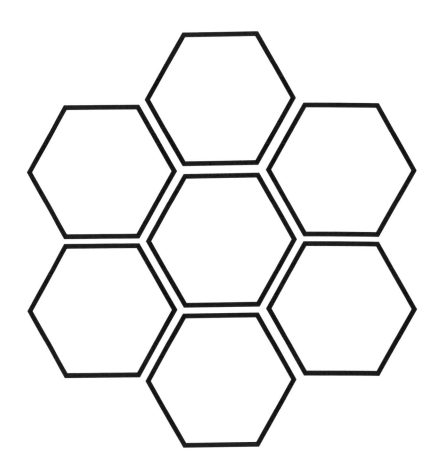

Looking Ahead

Real talk. This journal could have been hundreds of pages if I had let it. The truth is that you've just discovered 99% of what you need to know about yourself to keep the momentum going. And if I tried to get you through another 900 whatever pages of prompts, you'd probably give up, think I was crazy, or burn this book.

So let's bring it in real close for a moment to get clear on one thing.

YOU HAVE ALL THE ANSWERS INSIDE OF YOU

No one else on this planet can tell you what YOU need for YOU, except you. I'm not saying you shouldn't consult medical professionals, mental health specialists, financial advisors, or whoever is the expert in the advice you may be seeking. But what I am saying is that when it comes down to making a CHOICE about which direction to go with the information at your fingertips, the best person to turn to is yourself.

And the best way to build that trust and self-assurance in yourself and your own inner guidance is to touch base from time to time. Take yourself out on some sweet solo dates, bask in your awareness, and venture deep into journaling and self-discovery.

Momentum

What felt good during this process?

_____
_____
_____
_____

What needs more attention?

_____
_____
_____
_____

What are you ultimately seeking now?

_____
_____

What 3 daily steps/habits/practices can you start to make that happen?

_____
_____

How often do you want to come back to your reflections here? How will you remind yourself?

_____
_____
_____

Take 3

Caring for myself is not self-indulgence, it is self-preservation, and that is an act of political warfare.
-Audre Lorde

From Where I Begin

I am starting this journal on _____

I am currently _____ years old but I feel more like _____
and I think it's because _____
_____
_____

One thing I know for sure is that I am _____
and it allows me to _____

My hope is to discover _____

The biggest struggle for me right now is _____
and it often causes _____

The 3 things I am most happy about at this time:
1)_____
2)_____
3)_____

3 Things I know now that I didn't know a year ago:
1)_____
2)_____
3)_____

I know that if I choose to let go of _____
I will give myself freedom in the form of _____

Reflection

Last year around this time I was struggling with _____ and now I'm confident in _____

6 months ago I used to _____, now I _____

I don't give myself enough credit for how often I _____

I now realize that my relationship with _____ is/was causing _____

I found that many of my thoughts were focused on _____ _____ and I'd like to shift them toward _____

I know I have experienced growth because _____ _____ and it shows in how I _____

I find myself _____ much less and _____ much more.

If I had to choose a word or a theme for the past year, it would be _____ because _____ _____

Take Pause

Now that you've taken some time to reflect on your growth and awareness, take a deep breath and let it all marinate for a moment. You may want to put down this workbook and go for a walk or set a timer for 5 minutes to meditate or have a glass of water. Once you feel collected, use the space below to narrow your focus.

I have realized that I want to feel more _____
in my life because _____

Now more than ever, it is important that I focus on
_____
_____

I had no idea just how much _____
was affecting my daily life.

Circle the areas of your life below that feel good. Highlight the ones that you want to fuel, nourish, and grow.

Self-Love   Family   Friends   Boundaries   Support

Home   Health   Movement   Sleep   Self-Care   Relaxation

Trust   Work   Creativity   Spirituality   Organization

Nourishment   Environment   Emotional   Fun   Nature

Find Your Focus

As you continue through this guide you have several choices. To journey through it without barriers or to answer the remaining prompts with a specific lens in line with your goals and focus areas. There is no wrong or right way to continue. The beauty is that you can use this guide over and over again in a variety of ways. If you're craving more structure, the next few pages are for you.

Use the space below to write down the words you have highlighted on the previous page.

Find Your Focus Continued

This next step will help you get clear on which areas of your life you feel most energetically drawn to, in other words, the areas that you're feeling in your gut need your attention now more than ever. This part can be a bit tricky but I'm going to ask you to narrow down your choices to only two areas.

Area 1

What is lacking? What do you ultimately want? What changes if that happens for you?

_____
_____
_____
_____
_____
_____
_____
_____

Area 2

What is lacking? What do you ultimately want? What changes if that happens for you?

_____
_____
_____
_____
_____
_____
_____
_____

Harnessing Your Power

Congratulations, you're about to choose a focus! There may still be some resistance for you here and that's normal. Focusing in now will not limit you, it will help you gain a deep understanding and clarity on each area and section of your life in great detail. This gives you the power to eliminate confusion, self-doubt, and all of those nasty "what ifs" that can keep us up late at night. Once you have become clear on one at a time you can come back through this process once more. Go head, announce it, already!

I am choosing to focus on _____ and I know it's time because _____

I feel _____ and that's okay.

One thing I know for sure is that committing to this area of my life will allow me to finally _____ and _____

I am looking forward to this area allowing me to _____ and step into _____

I am afraid that diving deeper into this area of my life might mean _____ but I trust that _____

_____

Use this space to let go of any additional thoughts, worries, or concerns you need to release at this moment. This allows you to rid yourself of mental clutter and better focus on what you truly need. Do not worry about trying to solve them, simply write them down.

_____
_____
_____
_____
_____
_____
_____
_____
_____
_____
_____
_____
_____
_____
_____
_____
_____
_____
_____
_____
_____
_____
_____
_____
_____
_____
_____
_____
_____
_____

Beginnings

The hardest part about starting is _____
but it's easier when I _____

I am confident that if I _____
that I will be successful in _____

Right now it is important that I _____
so I can focus on _____

I am looking for _____
and I can find it by _____

I feel overwhelmed by the idea of _____
but I give myself permission to _____

In starting from where I am without judgment, I will be able
to _____

The biggest lie I keep telling myself is _____
and I've proven it's not true by _____

When I get overwhelmed I tend to _____
and I can take care of myself and this feeling by _____
_____

Dreams and reality
are opposites.
Action synthesizes
them.

- Assata Shakur

Preparation

It's important that I feel _____
in order to feel confident getting started.

In the past, it has been helpful to _____
before jumping into a new goal.

The biggest reason I want to _____
is to allow myself to _____

I feel less stressed when I _____
which allows me to _____

One way I could start tracking my to-do list is to _____
and then reward myself by _____

Everything I want to work on would feel a lot less overwhelming
if I made time to _____

I can create structure toward my desires by _____
and I will make this a priority by _____

A few things that I need help and direction on are _____
_____
and I can get help and find resource for this by _____
_____

You are your best thing.
— Toni Morrison

Intuition

I know something is off when I feel _____
_____ in my body.

There have been times my gut feeling has tried to tell me
_____ and I ignored it which led to
_____

The last time I trusted in my gut feeling, I _____
and it showed me _____

I often seek external validation in the form of _____
and it has made me feel _____

I also find that seeking external validation can cause me to
_____ and prevent me from
_____

There are times when I have to trust in myself over the
opinions or words of others, I can best do this by _____
_____

I don't need facts or hard logic to know when I _____
because _____

Trusting in myself means allowing myself to _____
even in the face of _____

Decision

When I feel overwhelmed by choice, it usually stems from a fear of _____

The biggest decision I ever made was _____ _____ and it helped me discover _____
_____

Choices feel difficult when I'm not paying attention to
_____
and I can change this by _____

I can trust myself more to make decisions that serve me by
_____

When in doubt, the best things that help me weigh my options are _____

Taking time to let go of others' expectations helps me make decisions rooted in _____
instead of _____

When I feel indecisive, it's important that I take time to
_____ and give myself enough time to
_____

Trust

It is important that I take time to _____
in a new relationship before I _____

I trust in my ability to _____
for myself because I know _____

If I spoke the words I speak to myself to others, I would feel
_____ about how they were being treated.

When I feel I need advice and no one is around, I know I can take time to _____
and it will give me the answers that I need.

In order for me to feel comfortable being my true self in front of others, I need to know _____
and I will know this by _____

I know that I cannot trust someone when _____
and I often have to remind myself of this by _____
_____

For me, trust means _____
and it's important that I keep this standard to myself because
_____

Connection

I find that I _____ need to be around people for _____ amount of time in order to feel like my best self.

When I think of community, I think of _____

I thrive when I am _____ people for an extended period of time.

Alone time makes me feel _____ and time with others makes me feel _____

Feeling connected means that I feel _____ and this usually happens when _____

I feel most connected to myself when I am _____ and the last time I made time for this was _____
_____

As I look ahead, it's important that I find connection for myself by _____
and reflecting on _____

I feel most alone when _____
and most connected when _____

When I think about the connections I currently have in life, in awareness, in creativity, and so forth, I want to make more time for _____

Acceptance

I am working on accepting that I _____
and it is helping me to see that _____

Acceptance means that I allow myself to _____
even in the face of _____

I am learning to _____ the things I
cannot change and _____
with the aspects of life that I can shift.

When things don't go my way I want to _____
_____
instead of _____

I will be able to make this a reality by regularly _____
_____

When I encounter things I cannot accept, I will assert my
boundaries by _____
and by honoring _____

To me, there is a big difference between acceptance and
_____. This distinction helps me see
_____

Creativity

Happiness researchers have discovered that we enter happy zones when we are focused and in the moment on a specific task. It's why knitting, drawing, coloring, crafting, or even playing strategic video games can make us feel at ease and enthralled in the process. Creating is important but the process of creating and being present can be even more so. Whatever you create, no matter how tactile, abstract, or imaginary, creates purpose in the process, and a deeply rooted sense of self-worth and self-efficacy is hidden in there as well. I encourage you to take time to create, not for the finished product alone, but also for the enjoyment of creating.

Creating for me means _____
and feeling _____
in the process.

I have always enjoyed the process of _____
and looking back I think it's because it truly allowed me to be able to _____
_____

Top projects I've LOVED the process of

_____
_____
_____
_____

Mindset

I tend to assume that I cannot _____
and it has limited me when _____
_____

I regularly tell myself _____
when starting a new challenge.

If I truly believed that I could _____
big things would change in how I _____
_____

My ability to _____
shows up in how I _____

When I doubt myself or my abilities, it's helpful to take time
to reflect on _____
and then take action by _____

I find a lot of comfort in _____
which can often hinder my ability to _____

I now choose to believe that I _____
and this will help me in _____
_____

Holy moly, that was a lot of introspective work. I don't know about you but the first few times I went through these, I needed to give my mind some time to exhale and take five. For that reason, this next section is geared to help you reset your brain -- kind of like smelling coffee beans after you smell too much perfume at Macy's.

I also love making lists like this to come back to years later. So if you use this on a yearly or regular basis, you'll have a ton of fun seeing how your answers change over time.

Currently, I'm...

Reading _____
Watching _____
Celebrating _____
Obsessed with _____
Wanting _____
Thinking about _____
Deciding _____
Feeling nostalgic _____
Wondering if _____
Debating _____
Craving _____
Creating _____
Dreaming _____
Brainstorming _____

Big Takeaways

Time to get real with yourself. What just happened back there? What's new? What has changed for you? What are you aware of now that you weren't before? Gush out all of the details here and make sure you get those juicy highlights down..........dang!

Looking Back

How did your area of focus effect your answers to the prompts?

_____
_____
_____
_____
_____

List out additional themes, words, or ideas that came to you during this process.

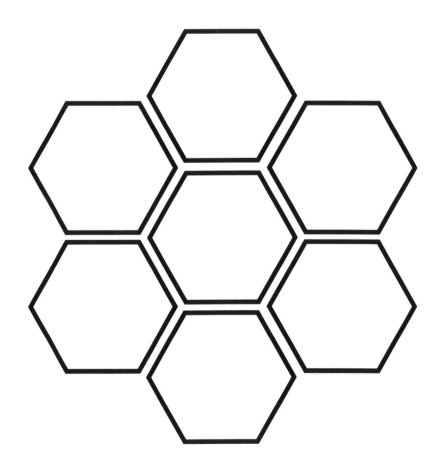

Looking Ahead

Real talk. This journal could have been hundreds of pages if I had let it. The truth is that you've just discovered 99% of what you need to know about yourself to keep the momentum going. And if I tried to get you through another 900 whatever pages of prompts, you'd probably give up, think I was crazy, or burn this book.

So let's bring it in real close for a moment to get clear on one thing.

YOU HAVE ALL THE ANSWERS INSIDE OF YOU

No one else on this planet can tell you what YOU need for YOU, except you. I'm not saying you shouldn't consult medical professionals, mental health specialists, financial advisors, or whoever is the expert in the advice you may be seeking. But what I am saying is that when it comes down to making a CHOICE about which direction to go with the information at your fingertips, the best person to turn to is yourself.

And the best way to build that trust and self-assurance in yourself and your own inner guidance is to touch base from time to time. Take yourself out on some sweet solo dates, bask in your awareness, and venture deep into journaling and self-discovery.

Momentum

What felt good during this process?

_____
_____
_____
_____

What needs more attention?

_____
_____
_____
_____

What are you ultimately seeking now?

_____
_____

What 3 daily steps/habits/practices can you start to make that happen?

_____
_____

How often do you want to come back to your reflections here? How will you remind yourself?

_____
_____

Take 4

_____

There are opportunities even in the most difficult moments.
-Wangari Maathai

From Where I Begin

I am starting this journal on _____

I am currently _____ years old but I feel more like _____
and I think it's because _____
_____
_____

One thing I know for sure is that I am _____
and it allows me to _____

My hope is to discover _____

The biggest struggle for me right now is _____
and it often causes _____

The 3 things I am most happy about at this time:
1)_____
2)_____
3)_____

3 Things I know now that I didn't know a year ago:
1)_____
2)_____
3)_____

I know that if I choose to let go of _____
I will give myself freedom in the form of _____

Reflection

Last year around this time I was struggling with _____ and now I'm confident in _____

6 months ago I used to _____, now I _____

I don't give myself enough credit for how often I _____

I now realize that my relationship with _____ is/was causing _____

I found that many of my thoughts were focused on _____ _____ and I'd like to shift them toward _____

I know I have experienced growth because _____ _____ and it shows in how I _____

I find myself _____ much less and _____ much more.

If I had to choose a word or a theme for the past year, it would be _____ because _____ _____

Take Pause

Now that you've taken some time to reflect on your growth and awareness, take a deep breath and let it all marinate for a moment. You may want to put down this workbook and go for a walk or set a timer for 5 minutes to meditate or have a glass of water. Once you feel collected, use the space below to narrow your focus.

I have realized that I want to feel more _____ in my life because _____

Now more than ever, it is important that I focus on

_____
_____

I had no idea just how much _____ was affecting my daily life.

Circle the areas of your life below that feel good. Highlight the ones that you want to fuel, nourish, and grow.

Self-Love   Family   Friends   Boundaries   Support

Home   Health   Movement   Sleep   Self-Care   Relaxation

Trust   Work   Creativity   Spirituality   Organization

Nourishment   Environment   Emotional   Fun   Nature

Find Your Focus

As you continue through this guide you have several choices. To journey through it without barriers or to answer the remaining prompts with a specific lens in line with your goals and focus areas. There is no wrong or right way to continue. The beauty is that you can use this guide over and over again in a variety of ways. If you're craving more structure, the next few pages are for you.

Use the space below to write down the words you have highlighted on the previous page.

Find Your Focus Continued

This next step will help you get clear on which areas of your life you feel most energetically drawn to, in other words, the areas that you're feeling in your gut need your attention now more than ever. This part can be a bit tricky but I'm going to ask you to narrow down your choices to only two areas.

Area 1

What is lacking? What do you ultimately want? What changes if that happens for you?

_____
_____
_____
_____
_____
_____
_____

Area 2

What is lacking? What do you ultimately want? What changes if that happens for you?

_____
_____
_____
_____
_____
_____
_____

Harnessing Your Power

Congratulations, you're about to choose a focus! There may still be some resistance for you here and that's normal. Focusing in now will not limit you, it will help you gain a deep understanding and clarity on each area and section of your life in great detail. This gives you the power to eliminate confusion, self-doubt, and all of those nasty "what ifs" that can keep us up late at night. Once you have become clear on one at a time you can come back through this process once more. Go head, announce it, already!

I am choosing to focus on _____
and I know it's time because _____

I feel _____ and that's okay.

One thing I know for sure is that committing to this area of my life will allow me to finally _____
and _____

I am looking forward to this area allowing me to _____
and step into _____

I am afraid that diving deeper into this area of my life might mean _____
but I trust that _____
_____

Use this space to let go of any additional thoughts, worries, or concerns you need to release at this moment. This allows you to rid yourself of mental clutter and better focus on what you truly need. Do not worry about trying to solve them, simply write them down.

_____
_____
_____
_____
_____
_____
_____
_____
_____
_____
_____
_____
_____
_____
_____
_____
_____
_____
_____
_____
_____
_____
_____
_____
_____
_____
_____
_____

Beginnings

The hardest part about starting is _____
but it's easier when I _____

I am confident that if I _____
that I will be successful in _____

Right now it is important that I _____
so I can focus on _____

I am looking for _____
and I can find it by _____

I feel overwhelmed by the idea of _____
but I give myself permission to _____

In starting from where I am without judgment, I will be able
to _____

The biggest lie I keep telling myself is _____
and I've proven it's not true by _____

When I get overwhelmed I tend to _____
and I can take care of myself and this feeling by _____
_____

It is better to fail in originality than to succeed in imitation.

-Herman Melville

Preparation

It's important that I feel _____
in order to feel confident getting started.

In the past, it has been helpful to _____
before jumping into a new goal.

The biggest reason I want to _____
is to allow myself to_____

I feel less stressed when I _____
which allows me to _____

One way I could start tracking my to-do list is to _____
and then reward myself by _____

Everything I want to work on would feel a lot less overwhelming
if I made time to _____

I can create structure toward my desires by _____
and I will make this a priority by _____

A few things that I need help and direction on are _____
_____
and I can get help and find resource for this by _____
_____

If you believe it will work out, you'll see opportunities. If you believe it won't, you will see obstacles.
— Wayne Dyer

Intuition

I know something is off when I feel _____
_____in my body.

There have been times my gut feeling has tried to tell me
_____ and I ignored it which led to
_____

The last time I trusted in my gut feeling, I _____
and it showed me _____

I often seek external validation in the form of _____
and it has made me feel _____

I also find that seeking external validation can cause me to
_____ and prevent me from
_____

There are times when I have to trust in myself over the
opinions or words of others, I can best do this by _____
_____

I don't need facts or hard logic to know when I _____
because _____

Trusting in myself means allowing myself to _____
even in the face of _____

Decision

When I feel overwhelmed by choice, it usually stems from a fear of _____

The biggest decision I ever made was _____
_____ and it helped me discover _____
_____

Choices feel difficult when I'm not paying attention to
_____
and I can change this by _____

I can trust myself more to make decisions that serve me by
_____

When in doubt, the best things that help me weigh my options are _____

Taking time to let go of others' expectations helps me make decisions rooted in _____
instead of _____

When I feel indecisive, it's important that I take time to
_____ and give myself enough time to
_____

Trust

It is important that I take time to _____
in a new relationship before I _____

I trust in my ability to _____
for myself because I know _____

If I spoke the words I speak to myself to others, I would feel
_____ about how they were
being treated.

When I feel I need advice and no one is around, I know I can
take time to _____
and it will give me the answers that I need.

In order for me to feel comfortable being my true self in front of
others, I need to know _____
and I will know this by _____

I know that I cannot trust someone when _____
and I often have to remind myself of this by _____
_____

For me, trust means _____
and it's important that I keep this standard to myself because
_____

Connection

I find that I _____ need to be around people for _____ amount of time in order to feel like my best self.

When I think of community, I think of _____

I thrive when I am _____ people for an extended period of time.

Alone time makes me feel _____
and time with others makes me feel _____

Feeling connected means that I feel _____
and this usually happens when _____

I feel most connected to myself when I am _____
and the last time I made time for this was _____
_____

As I look ahead, it's important that I find connection for myself by _____
and reflecting on _____

I feel most alone when _____
and most connected when _____

When I think about the connections I currently have in life, in awareness, in creativity, and so forth, I want to make more time for _____

Acceptance

I am working on accepting that I _____
and it is helping me to see that _____

Acceptance means that I allow myself to _____
even in the face of _____

I am learning to _____ the things I
cannot change and _____
with the aspects of life that I can shift.

When things don't go my way I want to _____
_____
instead of _____

I will be able to make this a reality by regularly _____
_____

When I encounter things I cannot accept, I will assert my
boundaries by _____
and by honoring _____

To me, there is a big difference between acceptance and
_____. This distinction helps me see
_____

Creativity

Happiness researchers have discovered that we enter happy zones when we are focused and in the moment on a specific task. It's why knitting, drawing, coloring, crafting, or even playing strategic video games can make us feel at ease and enthralled in the process. Creating is important but the process of creating and being present can be even more so. Whatever you create, no matter how tactile, abstract, or imaginary, creates purpose in the process, and a deeply rooted sense of self-worth and self-efficacy is hidden in there as well. I encourage you to take time to create, not for the finished product alone, but also for the enjoyment of creating.

Creating for me means _____
and feeling _____
in the process.

I have always enjoyed the process of _____
and looking back I think it's because it truly allowed me to be able to _____
_____

Top projects I've LOVED the process of

_____
_____
_____
_____

Mindset

I tend to assume that I cannot _____
and it has limited me when _____
_____

I regularly tell myself _____
when starting a new challenge.

If I truly believed that I could _____
big things would change in how I _____
_____

My ability to _____
shows up in how I _____

When I doubt myself or my abilities, it's helpful to take time
to reflect on _____
and then take action by _____

I find a lot of comfort in _____
which can often hinder my ability to _____

I now choose to believe that I _____
and this will help me in _____
_____

Holy moly, that was a lot of introspective work. I don't know about you but the first few times I went through these, I needed to give my mind some time to exhale and take five. For that reason, this next section is geared to help you reset your brain -- kind of like smelling coffee beans after you smell too much perfume at Macy's.

I also love making lists like this to come back to years later. So if you use this on a yearly or regular basis, you'll have a ton of fun seeing how your answers change over time.

Currently, I'm...

Reading _____
Watching _____
Celebrating _____
Obsessed with _____
Wanting _____
Thinking about _____
Deciding _____
Feeling nostalgic _____
Wondering if _____
Debating _____
Craving _____
Creating _____
Dreaming _____
Brainstorming _____

Big Takeaways

Time to get real with yourself. What just happened back there? What's new? What has changed for you? What are you aware of now that you weren't before? Gush out all of the details here and make sure you get those juicy highlights down..........dang!

Looking Back

How did your area of focus effect your answers to the prompts?

_____
_____
_____
_____
_____

List out additional themes, words, or ideas that came to you during this process.

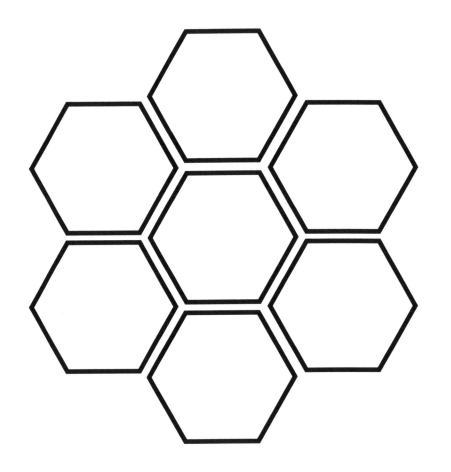

Looking Ahead

Real talk. This journal could have been hundreds of pages if I had let it. The truth is that you've just discovered 99% of what you need to know about yourself to keep the momentum going. And if I tried to get you through another 900 whatever pages of prompts, you'd probably give up, think I was crazy, or burn this book.

So let's bring it in real close for a moment to get clear on one thing.

YOU HAVE ALL THE ANSWERS INSIDE OF YOU

No one else on this planet can tell you what YOU need for YOU, except you. I'm not saying you shouldn't consult medical professionals, mental health specialists, financial advisors, or whoever is the expert in the advice you may be seeking. But what I am saying is that when it comes down to making a CHOICE about which direction to go with the information at your fingertips, the best person to turn to is yourself.

And the best way to build that trust and self-assurance in yourself and your own inner guidance is to touch base from time to time. Take yourself out on some sweet solo dates, bask in your awareness, and venture deep into journaling and self-discovery.

Momentum

What felt good during this process?

_____
_____
_____
_____

What needs more attention?

_____
_____
_____
_____

What are you ultimately seeking now?

_____
_____

What 3 daily steps/habits/practices can you start to make that happen?

_____
_____

How often do you want to come back to your reflections here? How will you remind yourself?

_____
_____
_____

Thanks for using this journal! If you enjoyed it, please consider leaving a review!

About The Creator

Sarah Steckler is an Author, Podcaster, Certified Health & Wellness Coach, Mindfulness Practitioner & Productivity Strategist who helps individuals feel more at ease and organized in their daily life through a combination of systems strategy & mindfulness practices.

She's been obsessed with her handsome husband ever since she met him at an Applebee's in 2011 and if you look her up on social media you'll soon find out how much she loves her bulldog, Bella.

If she has free time you can find her walking endlessly through the forest, getting excited over journal and planner supplies, or exploring her local library.

She also loves to learn and currently holds a Master's in Health & Wellness Coaching with a focus on Integrative Health Practices and a Bachelor's in Communications, along with a handful of online certifications she can't seem to stop enrolling in.

Listen to Sarah on the Mindful Productivity Podcast or contact her by visiting her blog or following her on Instagram @MindfulProductivityBlog

More resources, printables, and courses available at:

MindfulProductivityBlog.com

Made in the USA
Columbia, SC
04 March 2019